DEC 2019

GREAT ANIMAL COMEBACKS

SAVING THE GRAY WOLF

by Karen Latchana Kenney

po go

Ideas for Parents and Teachers

Pogo Books let children practice reading informational text while introducing them to nonfiction features such as headings, labels, sidebars, maps, and diagrams, as well as a table of contents, glossary, and index.

Carefully leveled text with a strong photo match offers early fluent readers the support they need to succeed.

Before Reading

- "Walk" through the book and point out the various nonfiction features. Ask the student what purpose each feature serves.
- Look at the glossary together. Read and discuss the words.

Read the Book

- Have the child read the book independently.
- Invite him or her to list questions that arise from reading.

After Reading

- Discuss the child's questions. Talk about how he or she might find answers to those questions.
- Prompt the child to think more. Ask: Have you heard about gray wolves? After reading this book, what more would you like to learn about them?

Pogo Books are published by Jump!
5357 Penn Avenue South
Minneapolis, MN 55419
www.jumplibrary.com

Library of Congress Cataloging-in-Publication Data

Names: Kenney, Karen Latchana, author.
Title: Saving the gray wolf / by Karen Latchana Kenney.
Description: Minneapolis, MN : Jump!, Inc., [2019] |
Series: Great animal comebacks | Audience: Age 7-10.
Includes index.
Identifiers: LCCN 2018033356 (print)
LCCN 2018035822 (ebook)
ISBN 9781641282857 (ebook)
ISBN 9781641282840 (hardcover : alk. paper)
Subjects: LCSH: Gray wolf–Conservation–
Juvenile literature. Wolves–Conservation–
Juvenile literature.
Classification: LCC QL737.C22 (ebook)
LCC QL737.C22 K46 2019 (print) | DDC 599.773–dc23
LC record available at https://lccn.loc.gov/2018033356

Editor: Jenna Trnka
Designer: Anna Peterson

Photo Credits: Ana Gram/Shutterstock, cover, 18;
Kjetil Kolbjornsrud/Shutterstock, 1; SERGEI BRIK/
Shutterstock, 3; twphotos/iStock, 4; Andyworks/iStock,
5; Warren Metcalf/Shutterstock, 6-7; Gallatin Historical
Museum, 8-9; Frank Fichtmuller/iStock, 10-11; labrlo/
iStock, 12; Tom Uhlman/Alamy, 13; Jim Cumming/
Shutterstock, 14-15; LuRay Parker/USFWS National
Digital Library, 16-17; Geoffrey Kuchera/Shutterstock,
19 (background); A.von Dueren/Shutterstock, 19
(foreground); Debbie Steinhauser/Shutterstock, 20-21;
creativex/Shutterstock, 23.

Printed in the United States of America at
Corporate Graphics in North Mankato, Minnesota.

TABLE OF CONTENTS

CHAPTER 1
WOLVES IN TROUBLE

It is dusk. A gray wolf raises her muzzle. She lets out a long howl. She calls to her **pack**. It is time to hunt.

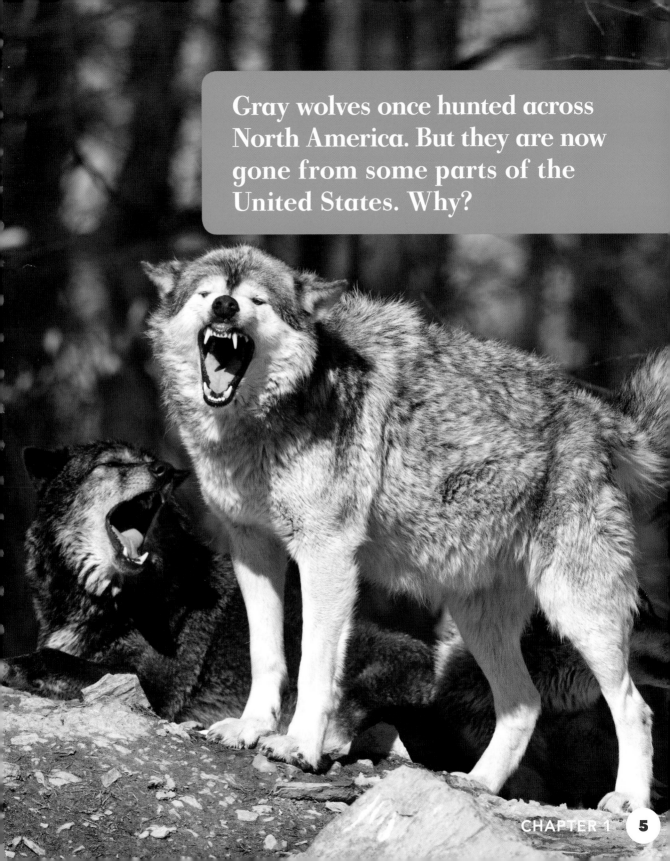

Gray wolves once hunted across North America. But they are now gone from some parts of the United States. Why?

They were plentiful before Europeans settled across North America. Settlers killed the wolves' **prey** for food.

And they hunted many of the wolves, too. Why? Settlers were afraid of them. They wanted to protect their **livestock**. These farm animals were easy prey for wolves.

wolfer

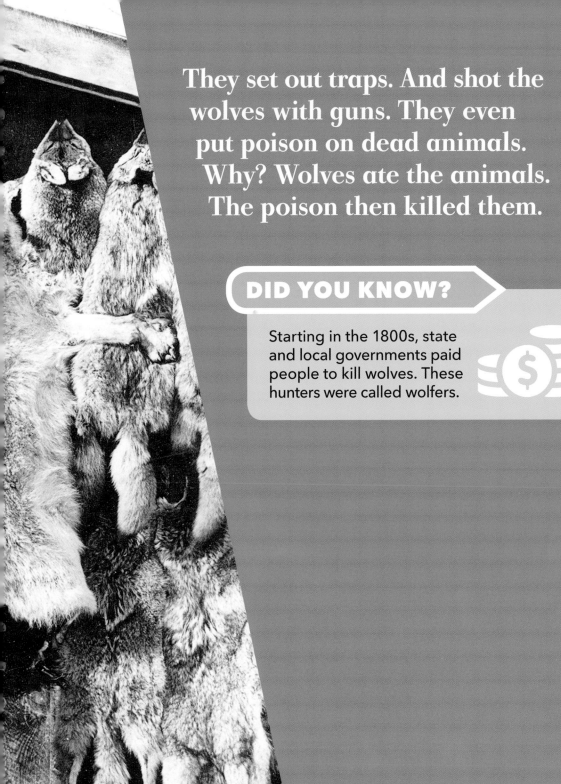

They set out traps. And shot the wolves with guns. They even put poison on dead animals. Why? Wolves ate the animals. The poison then killed them.

DID YOU KNOW?

Starting in the 1800s, state and local governments paid people to kill wolves. These hunters were called wolfers.

Gray wolves thrived before **overhunting**. One place was Yellowstone **National Park**. But the last ones in the park were killed in the 1920s. They had to be saved.

DID YOU KNOW?

Gray wolves don't have any **predators** in the wild. Only humans. Alaska and parts of Canada have large **populations** of gray wolves. Why? Few people live in these areas.

Yellowstone National Park

CHAPTER 2

SAVING THE WOLVES

Gray wolves are **apex predators**. They are at the top of the **food chain**.

They hunt many animals. Even large ones. Like what? Bison, moose, and deer. Wolves keep these populations from growing too large. Why is this important? They keep other animals and plants in balance, too.

By the early 1970s, gray wolf packs were gone from many states. Just a few hundred were left in northern Minnesota and Michigan.

A law helped save them. It passed in 1973. What was it? The **Endangered Species** Act. It made it illegal to kill or hurt wolves.

DID YOU KNOW?

Packs usually have up to 15 wolves. Young adult wolves decide to stay or leave the pack. If they leave, they join a different pack. Or start a new one.

A **conservation** plan was also made. The U.S. government formed a team. What was it called? The Northern Rocky Mountain Wolf Recovery Team. The team came up with a plan in 1980. It would bring gray wolves back to some places.

Where would the wolves come from? Canada. From 1995 to 1997, they were released in Yellowstone and Idaho. The packs grew. And the wolves helped these areas.

CHAPTER 3
WOLF PACKS TODAY

Today, wolf packs roam parts of the United States. A pack's leaders are the mother and father. They raise **pups**.

den

pup

A mother gives birth to four to six pups in the **den**. The pups grow into big wolves.

Gray wolves were saved. But hunting is still allowed in some areas, such as Alaska and Canada. People also move into their **habitats**.

We need gray wolves. They keep nature in balance. With our help, their howls can still be heard. How can you help them continue their comeback?

TAKE A LOOK!

Today, around 5,500 wolves live in the lower 48 states. Between 8,000 to 11,000 live in Alaska. Around 60,000 gray wolves live in Canada.

NORTH AMERICA

■ = known gray wolf populations

■ = may have gray wolf populations

ACTIVITIES & TOOLS

TOP OF THE FOOD CHAIN

Gray wolves are at the top of their food chain. They eat many animals, such as deer, bison, and rabbits. These animals eat grass and other plants. Draw a pyramid or web that shows how this food chain works. Draw the grass at the bottom. Where do the deer, bison, and rabbit belong? Where does the gray wolf belong?

Now try this with a different ecosystem and apex predator. Search online to find another apex predator. Fill in the pyramid to show its food chain.

GLOSSARY

apex predators: Predators at the top of a food chain that are not hunted by any other animal.

conservation: The protection of something, such as animals and wildlife.

den: The home of a wild animal.

endangered species: A plant or animal that is in danger of becoming extinct.

food chain: An ordered arrangement of animals and plants in which each feeds on the one below it in the chain.

habitats: The places and natural conditions in which animals or plants live.

livestock: Animals that are kept or raised on a farm or ranch.

national park: A large section of land that is protected by the federal government for people to visit and to preserve wildlife.

overhunting: Hunting an animal excessively to the point that the animal becomes scarce.

pack: A group of animals that hunts and lives together.

populations: The total numbers of living things in certain areas.

predators: Animals that hunt other animals for food.

prey: Animals that are hunted by other animals for food.

pups: Young wolves.

INDEX

TO LEARN MORE

Finding more information is as easy as 1, 2, 3.

① Go to www.factsurfer.com

② Enter "savingthegraywolf" into the search box.

③ Click the "Surf" button to see a list of websites.

FACT SURFER